# Foreword

The Royal Commission into the Criminal Justice System sponsored a series of more than twenty projects looking at a wide range of issues some of which are of relevance to policing and others slightly less so.

Although these papers are widely available, their sheer number and con-current production with major reports on law-enforcement issues (including the Royal Commission report itself) could mean that the research papers may be over-looked by busy police decision-makers.

The Police Research Group has therefore prepared this paper drawing out some police-relevant findings from the research. The recommendations made by the Royal Commission in their Report, published in July 1993 are currently being studied by government.

I M BURNS
*Deputy Under Secretary of State*
*Home Office,*
*September 1993*

# Contents

# ROYAL COMMISSION RESEARCH PAPERS
# A POLICING PERSPECTIVE

Jane Hirst

POLICE RESEARCH SERIES: PAPER NO.6
LONDON: HOME OFFICE POLICE DEPARTMENT

Editor: Gloria Laycock
Home Office Police Research Group
50 Queen Anne's Gate
London SW1H 9AT

**Police Research Series**

The Home Office Police Research Group (PRG) was formed in 1992 to carry out and manage research in the social and management sciences relevant to the work of the police service. The terms of reference for the Group include the requirement to identify and disseminate good policing practice.

The aim of the Police Research series is to present results of externally funded studies, and those carried out by the Police Research Group, in a way that will inform policy and practice throughout the police service.

A parallel series of papers on crime prevention is also published by PRG, as is a periodical on policing research called 'Focus'.

ISBN 1-85893-096-0

# Executive Summary

- The Royal Commission to review the criminal justice system sponsored a series of research studies on various aspects of the criminal justice process.

- The studies were carried out in a very short time frame. In order to meet the deadline, some studies were based on limited samples, so raising questions on methodological grounds about the results.

- This paper concentrates on those research findings and recommendations which have a policing interest. It ignores issues from the research eg forensic science which have a less direct impact on police and policing.

- Readers are alerted to the status of these recommendations as coming from researchers, not the Commission. For the issues covered, this paper links the research topics and findings to the discussion and recommendations of the Royal Commission.

- Some examples of the issues contained in this report are:
  - the notice for detained persons
  - fitness for interview
  - supervision of investigations
  - interview techniques and summaries
  - right to silence
  - reliability of confession evidence alone

- Police officers were found to be good at identifying the most obviously disabled and vulnerable detainees requiring the presence of a supporting adult during interview, but this was, nevertheless, only about one quarter of those who the researchers judged to require assistance. Self-identification by detainees raised this figure to 80%.

- Only 41% of a study sample of detainees completely understood their rights as presented to them in the form of the official 'Notice to Detained Persons'. The study trialled a revised notice that was fully understood by all with at least low average intelligence.

- Police supervision, especially in the CID, was observed to be weak, so increasing the risk of possible miscarriages of justice. The researchers recommend a greater supervisory role for sergeants, and a new ad-hoc Quality Control Unit to monitor standards of efficiency and probity in investigation.

- Police interviewing techniques were criticised because the researchers observed officers using a range of manipulative and persuasive ploys in effecting confessions. More training was recommended to ensure that interviews are directed to information gathering rather than manipulative questioning.

- One half of police interview summaries were found to fail as a record of interview because they were misleading or lacked detail. Civilian input into the process saved money but did not noticeably improve the quality of the summaries.

- Detainees invoking their right to silence were found to affect the outcome of very few cases. A legally represented detainee was more than twice as likely to invoke the right to silence than an unrepresented detainee.

- Few convictions were found to depend on confession evidence alone. The researcher argued, on this basis, that confession evidence should only be admitted if it were corroborated.

- The paper links the research findings to the Royal Commission's report.

# List of Tables

# 1. Introduction

In June 1991 the Government set up a Royal Commission to review the criminal justice system in England and Wales.[1] (The full terms of reference are set out in Appendix A.) The Royal Commission reported in June 1993.

The Royal Commission on Criminal Justice, *Report*, London, HMSO, July 1993.

The Royal Commission funded a series of research studies to assist in its deliberations. Twenty-three reports have now been published covering aspects of police investigations, the role of experts in criminal proceedings, case preparation and the court process. The various studies made recommendations on a wide sweep of, in the main, detailed operating procedures of the criminal justice process. The recommendations were not, of course, binding on the Royal Commission which chose to incorporate some of them into its recommendations and to ignore or modify others.

The studies are numbered, and their titles and authors listed in Appendix B. Studies are referred to throughout this report by their number.

The research studies were prepared in a very short time frame. To meet this timetable, some investigations were based on surveys designed for another purpose, so raising questions about the research on methodological grounds. (See, for example, Study 3). Some researchers set up new surveys, but based them, in effect, on a narrow geographical area (eg. Study 11 on Forensic Science). In some cases the limited sample did not weaken a general conclusion. For example, Study 2 researched police transcripts of tape-recorded interviews. The researcher took his sample from those police forces he was advised were most likely to produce good quality summaries. If he was right in this selection, when he found that practice in these forces fell short of expectations, the generally dismal conclusions could justly be extrapolated to the whole. But in other studies the limited sample sometimes side-stepped the diversity of experience and operational procedures in the various forces in England and Wales. Accordingly it cannot be assumed that practices described as 'good' are universally implemented, or that those recommended for adoption are not already fixedly in place in some forces. Such disparity between forces in effect means that it is difficult, without further investigation, either to determine the extent of changes necessary to implement the recommendations, or the total resource costs of such changes.

This paper is targeted at a readership with an interest in policing. It focuses on a selection of research findings and recommendations of relevance to police. It does not pretend to provide a balanced precis or study guide to the Royal Commission research papers, and deliberately fails to comment on issues canvassed by the studies but with no direct or indirect policing implication.

Most of the results and recommendations discussed in this paper relate to changed or additional practices. They arise from a critical examination of the operation of the whole Criminal Justice System rather than of the police itself. Consequently, many of the recommendations for changes in police practices (eg to documentation) are made to enable other participants in the system eg CPS or defence counsel better to meet their remit.

As many of the changes recommended have resource implications, they perhaps foreshadow a series of funding and resource battles that lie beyond the brief of both the Commission and of this paper. Because of the diversity of policing practices in England and Wales, however, the recommendations, and therefore the resource will not apply equally to all Constabularies.

The Royal Commission research papers examine aspects of the criminal justice process from a suspect's initial detention for questioning to Crown Court proceedings. This paper, in keeping with its police emphasis, focuses on the detention and the interviewing/investigation process. It is in this context that this paper identifies a number of police-relevant issues covered by the Royal Commission research and, for each:

- *selects* from the Commission's research studies those results and recommendations that would, if, implemented, mean *changes in present police practices*

- explains *how* the researchers developed their recommendations; and

- spells out some *implications* for policing if the recommendations of the research were accepted, especially for

  - resources management and

  - skills development

- links the research to the findings and recommendations of the Royal Commission.

## 2. The pre-interview phase

Problems in deciding the suitability of detainees for interview were touched on in Studies 6, 7 and 12. The recommendations cover the related but different issues of the detainee's fitness for interview and his understanding of his rights within the interview process.

### Notice to Detained Persons

A concern that a miscarriage of justice may occur if detainees do not fully understand their rights as presented to them in the form of the official "Notice to Detained Persons" (hereafter referred to as "the notice") underlies the discussion in Study 7. Drawing on already published and new research, the study concludes that understanding by the detained person of the presently-used notice is poor, whether it is presented to the detainee as a written document or by word-of-mouth. The research also shows that the higher the intellectual ability of the subject the higher is his understanding of the notice. However, one study suggests that the notice as it presently stands can only be fully understood by a person with an IQ of 105 or more (ie only 40% of the population). It seems unlikely that detainees could understand all the provisions of the notice if the outcome of crude IQ testing of a sample of real detainees in Study 7 is representative of police detainees. The average IQ of this group tested as 82 (compared with the national average of 100); this included a third of the sample below 75 (ie technically intellectually impaired).

The researchers (Study 7) tested an experimental notice. This proved to be better understood by the test sample of 100 persons than the present version. Compared with only a 41% understanding of the present document, (only one of the sample fully understood all its provisions) the experimental notice was 72% understood by all subjects, and fully understood by all with a low average intellectual ability or above.

Accordingly, the research recommended that the notice be changed to make the issues it encompasses more comprehensible to detainees (Study 12). The Royal Commission accepted this view, and recommended pilot testing for the experimental, simplified version of the notice, proposed in Study 7, (Royal Commission recommendation 52). Two members of the Royal Commission also recommended that the Home Office experiment with showing suspects a video recording to explain their rights. This additional recommendation was not canvassed by the research.

The introduction of a simplified notice would appear to be a costless recommendation for an improvement to policing procedures, with the small exception of monitoring the trial studies, evaluating the results and eventually reprinting sets of notices. A video alternative would, however, have significant cost implications for forces.

**Fit for Interview?**

The discussion on determining fitness for interview arose from a concern that miscarriages of justice may occur if police officers fail to identify vulnerable suspects requiring the presence of a supportive adult during interview.

In the sample of police detainees investigated in Study 12, the researchers estimated that 15% met the (admittedly poorly defined) PACE criteria for requiring the presence of an appropriate adult during interview. This was almost four times the 4% identified by the custody officers in charge of the detainees. Further, after taking into account additional psychological testing, the researchers found the proportion of detainees in the study requiring a supporting adult exceeded 20% of the sample.

The study observed that while police officers were very good at identifying the most disabled and vulnerable suspects for interview support, they were less adept at recognising depressive mental illness and mental handicap (which can often be disguised by a facade of seemingly competent social functioning).

Various measures better to identify vulnerable individuals in need of a supportive adult during interview and/or a detainee's suitability for interview were suggested in the studies.

These included

- placing part of the onus for identifying the need for a supporting adult on the detainee himself, through his responses to direct questioning by the custody officer (Studies 12 and 7);
- developing an operational definition of mental disorder and vulnerability together with clearer guidelines for police officers to decide whether an appropriate adult should be present during an interview (Study 12);
- training officers to be more skilled at identifying vulnerable individuals, including the mentally ill (Study 12).

The research tested the effectiveness of suspects identifying their own need for a supporting adult. Eighty per cent of the study group judged by the researchers to be eligible for this adult support either because of intellectual difficulties or severe reading difficulties, correctly self-identified when prompted by police questioning. Only 2% wrongly self- identified. This outcome suggests that a higher proportion of those 'vulnerable' detainees requiring adult support during interview will be apparent if detainees are asked.

A working definition and clear guidelines of mental disorder and vulnerability would undoubtedly assist police officers in deciding whether an appropriate adult should be present with a detainee during interview. Still, even ignoring the difficulty of devising such guidelines, it is unlikely that they would be effective in pin-pointing all vulnerable persons. Study 12 specifically notes the inherent difficulties in identifying some types of mental illness and mental handicap, which would be unlikely to be overcome even with the most sophisticated guidelines.

The Commission's report noted that "other means must ... be sought of identifying those people who need the services of an appropriate adult" (paragraph 40, page 34). The Royal Commission did not, however, grasp the nettle on this issue. Instead, in recommendation 72, discussed in paragraphs 84 (page 43) and 86 (page 44) it advocates the establishment of a review to consider all aspects of the use of "appropriate adults" including "whether the police need clearer guidelines about the criteria to be employed when considering the need for an appropriate adult."

Studies 12 and 7 offer conflicting advice over which police officer/s should decide on a detainee's fitness for interview. Study 12 implied continuence of the present practice that the custody officer decide a detainee's fitness for interview. That study noted that specialist custody officers are more effective at such decision-making, and recommended that the "custody officer" be a specialist position.

Study 7, without supporting empirical evidence or argument, recommended that the investigating officer decide on the fitness of a suspect for interview, supported by advice from mental-health specialists, if required.

There would be significant cost differences (mainly in training costs) between these two options. Even so, the cost effect for a particular force would depend on its particular present staffing practices and so could not be extrapolated across all constabularies. The inconsistent advice on which officer should decide on a detainee's fitness for interview was not addressed by the Commission.

Similarly, the Commission's report made no comment on the recommendation from Study 6 for standardised custody record documentation between all forces to record call out requests for a police surgeon. The researcher had suggested this development so that it would always be apparent if advice had been sought from a police surgeon on a suspect's fitness for interview.

# 3. The investigation

Since 1984, the Police and Criminal Evidence Act (PACE) has strongly influenced the conduct of police investigations. The implementation of the Act's provisions has dampened the loudest allegations of improperly conducted investigations that may imply or result in a miscarriage of justice. Still a number of controversial issues remain and are canvassed in the Commission's research papers.

The Commission's terms of reference specifically charge it with examining the degree of supervision of police investigations. Studies 4 and 5 cover this issue, but both papers developed their recommendations after observing CID investigations of so-called serious crime. The papers can be thought of as risk analyses, examining the institution and modus operandi of the CID, to identify those factors which most risk miscarriages of justice. In addition, Study 21 focuses on quality control failures in the CID as potential, but widely unacknowledged, causes of miscarriages of justice. Accordingly, the studies' recommendations best apply in the CID environment.

## CID Ethos

All studies criticise the so-called CID ethos, and conclude that it opens investigations to risks of miscarriage of justice. Studies 4 and 5 found that the CID ethos involves a set of broad working practices which are individualistic, competitive and results oriented, where supervision is minimal and more inspirational or charismatic than controlling, and corners are often cut. The CID officer's self-image is as part of an elite. Study 5 opines that these attitudes have traditionally been combined with a macho hard-drinking life-style (although the researcher acknowledges that drink-driving legislation has undermined some of these excesses) where socialisation into the job was regarded as important as formal training. The detective training itself is criticised in Studies 4 and 5 as giving too little attention to good practice and procedures with the result that new detectives learn by watching more experienced officers on the job, and existing bad practices are perpetuated. Study 21 criticises force-wide training for failing to acknowledge that errors may occur, and so failing to teach strategies to minimise such errors.

The ideological thrust of the Strategic Policy Document published in 1990 by the Association of Chief Police Officers (ACPO), offered support for the concept of 'quality of service'. The practical adoption of some of the principles expounded by ACPO, although driven more by concerns about management effectiveness and efficiency than possible malpractice, has eroded some traditional CID attitudes. For example, closer working links between CID and uniform branches undermine CID exclusivity. Still, Study 5 found CID attitudes sufficiently entrenched to recommend implementation of changes in practice to diminish the risks inherent in the present system, and to monitor the quality and integrity of investigations. Those recommendations include:

- fostering an attitudinal change within police forces so that police acknowledge the existence of a potential problem in conducting investigations;

- attacking the CID culture ie the macho and élitist CID stance by, for example, limiting the term of CID appointments and ensuring a broader range of persons is appointed to CID, through strict adherence to the principles of Equal Employment Opportunity (EEO);

- reducing the pressure on investigating officers to obtain a result. (Sometimes this pressure is force-generated; sometimes it comes from the press or other outside influences. In this latter case, the researcher suggests, the investigating officer requires shielding from the external pressure for a result;)

- bridging the divide between uniform and CID by, for example, more use of mixed squads, and placing management of the CID under a central force control rather than a dedicated CID hierarchy;

- clarifying responsibilities and separate functions in investigations, so that no one officer is personally responsible for the outcome of an investigation;

- seeking new investigation techniques to diminish reliance on uncorroborated confession. The study comments on the informer/surveillance model of pro-active investigation as preferable to, and having more inherent safeguards for criminal justice, than the re-active investigation/interview styles;

- changing the managerial culture so that equal emphasis is placed on ensuring procedural and legal compliancies as on 'getting results';

- establishing a system of complete quality control based on independence and randomness. This would work through a specialist Quality Control Unit able randomly to check the procedural and legal propriety of an officer's work rather than just his/her effectiveness;

- introducing a probationary period for detectives during which they will be closely monitored and must show that they perform tasks to an acceptable standard of clearly articulated good practice. Such a system should reinforce formal training, and undermine the present practice of new detectives acquiring the bad habits, whether of omission or commission, of their more experienced colleagues.

With the exception of the last two suggestions, these recommendations and the observations of police practice from which they were derived, are not new. Many of the suggested practices are already in place in some but not all the forces in England and Wales.

Study 21 also looked at the risks for CID investigations inherent in the present system, by focusing on human error. This research considers the human side of quality control in CID investigations. A sample of 60 cases of admitted error in the police handling of criminal matters was studied. (Twelve of the cases had been identified by the CPS, the remainder by the police officers involved.) The findings suggested that human error, rather than conscious rule breaking or police impropriety was the cause of most failures in quality control by police. In 17 of the 60 cases, the admitted errors led to failures of prosecution.

Consistent with Studies 4 and 5, Study 21 targets the CID ethos. This ethos, the report notes, both militates against the development of a quality control system to minimise human error, and also contributes to ensuring that mistakes caused by human error are hidden and ignored (unless they become the centre of disciplinary action or outside intervention).

Yet human error occurs. The research provides evidence that individual officers recognise this, and under the cover of complete confidentiality, as was provided by the researchers of Study 21, were willing to admit to making mistakes. However institutionally, the CID, and in a wider sphere the other elements of the Criminal Justice system (the Courts and the CPS in particular), do not yet adopt a reasonable view of quality control failures in investigation.

Acknowledging that it offers only a pilot investigation of these issues, and possibly also as a warning in accepting the fine details of the research without question, Study 21 recommends further research to test and refine its findings.
It also recommends

- establishing an independent confidential reporting system for quality control failures;

- changing training for all operational police and police supervisors to make them aware of the circumstances most likely to promote errors and how to avoid them;

- the courts and the CPS adapting to a reasonable view of quality control failures in investigation. Systems must be introduced so that errors can be brought to notice and corrected, rather than be hidden and become the cause of malpractice allegations.

Study 21 also notes that the present culture within the CID prevents the introduction of effective quality control measures. If eventually, a cultural change does occur, the study recommends that stress management, now seen as a welfare measure, should become an integral part of total quality management.

In effect, the recommendations of the researchers of Studies 4, 5 and 21 fall into two categories:

(1) wide-ranging changes in attitude and corporate philosophy; and

(2) radical changes in the institutional environment of policing that would be necessary to effect the recommended attitudinal changes.

The Commission's recommendations are less explicit than the researchers'. Still, they are also directed at changing the institutional environment of detective work. To that end, the Commission has recommended:

- "... an overhaul of detective training and of training in investigations ... " (Recommendation 29)

- that "police forces ... put their methods of select(ing) officers for Criminal Investigations Departments onto a more formal basis linked to clear job descriptions" (Recommendation 30)

- and that "police performance should not be assessed unduly on the basis of arrest or conviction rates" (Recommendation 31).

And, as always, when major institutional changes are mooted, the implications in resource costs are never immediately fully apparent; more work will be required to determine the management and resource costs to individual constabularies of implementing specific recommendations.

## Supervision

The discussion on supervision of investigations is also largely based on observation of CID practice. Within this environment, the researchers distinguish between larger and smaller cases. The normal conduct of a large case, especially one for which investigations are managed using the HOLMES system, contains a range of built-in guides and checks that deflect most criticism of potential miscarriages of justice. In particular, no one officer has reason or opportunity to fabricate evidence. Yet, Study 4 observes, most investigations are smaller-scale and are carried out by relatively junior police officers working in small teams and without any direct supervision to give guidance or control.

In this context Study 4 recommends:

- an upgraded sergeant's role to facilitate supervision; and

- supervision based on responsibility and grounded on rank.

Such recommendations have arisen from an observation of CID practices where the sergeant has a heavy case load and is first among equals, rather than a supervisor assigned a specific role, as often occurs in uniformed policing. Questions may be asked whether these recommendations can be applied to the force as a whole, though the researchers have implied that their recommendations can be generalised in this way.

Study 4 neither argues the disadvantages of inadequate supervision of daily detective activity nor the perceived advantages of increased supervision by sergeants. However, Study 5 sets out more cogently the case for increasing the supervisory responsibilities of detective sergeants. The researcher argues that present supervisory practices are weak and this increases the risk of possible miscarriages of justice. Contributing factors noted are:

- the sergeant's role as supervisor is undermined by his heavy case load, and together with the commitment to 'get results' may mean that he is as susceptible as any detective to 'bend the rules' rather than to act as a supervisory brake on any such tendencies;

- the constant drain on supervisory staff for specialist roles means frequent short-term 'acting-up'; an acting supervisor finds hard decisions, such as disciplining fellow officers, even harder to make; and

- the nature of police work makes police supervision difficult in any event because so much of it is done out of the eye of the supervisor.

Study 5 suggests that lack of supervision is not unique to CID but is an example of a more general quality management malaise. The researcher's solution to the immediate CID problem is to upgrade the sergeants' supervisory role by making them responsible for supervising a specific group of officers (as is being introduced in the Metropolitan Police). This issue, discussed by the Royal Commission in paragraph 59 on page 20 of the report, underlies Recommendation 28 which suggests that ".. sergeants should work as supervisors as well as having their own caseloads, and detective sergeants should be held accountable within reason for the performance of the detective constables under their supervision."

For those forces and CIDs where the supervisory deployment of sergeants would be innovatory, it would entail major changes in the job description of that rank, which may well generate some management and organisational problems. The practicality of requiring of a sergeant a supervisory role without any corresponding relief from their case load is questioned by the research findings that the sergeant's case load undermines his supervisory role. Besides, if sergeants were able effectively to carry the additional responsibility for the performance of constables under their supervision, it seems pertinent to inquire whether the small pay differential between constable and sergeant would adequately reflect the much greater differential in responsibility between the two and the significant increase in work-load for the sergeant.

In addition, Study 5 recommends the introduction of a Quality Control Unit, ie an ad-hoc, uninvited, officer-level inspection unit to monitor standards of efficiency and probity (as noted in the section above).

The nature of the proposed quality control units is not well-articulated beyond its principles, but it may be predicted that some interesting personnel management issues would require settling before such units gained general police acceptance. The Royal Commission did not incorporate this research recommendation into their recommendations.

# 4. Interviews

The recording of interviews under PACE has quieted the most telling criticisms that the interview process causes or fosters miscarriages of justice. Any residual doubts about police malpractice in interviews have, therefore, been focused on those interviews which occur outside the structured procedures of a police station interview room. Studies 13 and 22 touch on this issue.

Study 22 distinguishes between "interviewing" and "questioning" by quoting from the *Notes for Guidance* in Code C to the PACE Act.

> "An interview is the questioning of a person regarding his involvement or suspected involvement in a criminal offence or offences. Questioning a person only to obtain information or his explanation of the facts or in the ordinary course of the officer's duties does not constitute an interview for the purpose of this code. Neither does questioning which is confined to the proper and effective conduct of a search."

Study 13 uses the terms "questioning" and "interviewing" interchangeably, and so draws attention to the practical difficulties in distinguishing between the two terms. Study 22 also observed police officers' confusion in distinguishing between the two, and their uncertainty over the circumstances where interviewing outside the police station is permissible. In essence, with a few exceptions, under PACE, interviewing outside the station is effectively outlawed, yet questioning is still frequently required. But initial reluctance by some officers to admit that any verbal exchanges at all occurred between police officers and detainees outside the police station is further evidence of police officer confusion over what is and is not permissible.

The Royal Commission, in its report, noted the confusion inherent in Code C's guidance (see paragraph 10, page 27 of the Commission's report) and recommended "... that this apparent confusion be clarified when Code C is next revised" (see Recommendation 38).

Of the sample of 641 suspects interviewed by police in Study 22, 31% were questioned by police before arriving at the police station. A very similar 32.5% of the sample of 532 suspects interviewed in Study 13 were "interviewed" by police prior to arrest. Study 22 also identified 52 (8.1%) of its detainees who were "interviewed", as distinct from "questioned" before arrival at the police station. In most cases the statements made outside the station were repeated during a tape-recorded interview at the station, and the researcher found no evidence, direct or indirect, of undue police influence being brought to bear on a detainee during these earlier interviews.

The main finding of the paper was the observation that interviews inside the police station cannot stand in isolation from all that has gone before. Interviewing is a process, not a one-off event, but present procedures fail to recognise this.

In acknowledgement that exchanges occur between police and detainees outside the interview room as part of the investigation process, the researcher recommends that all officers carry portable tape recorders and record all exchanges with both suspects and witnesses. In the research study, officers admitted to carrying tape recorders in 6.6% of cases. Tape recording of all exchanges would also remove doubts cast over conversations between the detainee and the arresting officer. This innovation could never entirely prevent "the off the record chat", but should contribute to:

- recognition that interviewing as it occurs in police investigations is a process rather than a one-off event;

- the investigative process, and intelligence gathering, in the interviewing of witnesses; and

- removing the current over-emphasis on interviews with the detainee in the police station.

While the Royal Commission is not entirely convinced that tape recording will solve all problems associated with verbal interchanges outside the police station, (see discussion in paragraphs 11-13, pages 27-28 of the Royal Commission report), the report does conclude that:

"extending tape recordings as far as practicable to situations that arise outside the police station will represent a significant addition to the current range of safeguards for suspects and police officers alike".

In accord with that sentiment, Recommendation 39 states that:

"If the experimental project in Essex demonstrates the feasibility of tape-recording exchanges between suspects and police officers outside the police station, extensions to the PACE codes should be considered to cover what should and should not be permissible between arrest outside the police station and arrival at it."

At the same time, the research study questions the introduction of video technology to record police interviewing practices. It observes that such recording would place further emphasis on the "police station interview" which the study has identified as only one element of the police interviewing process. Accordingly, this researcher concludes that video recording of police station interviews should not take precedence over sound recording the full sequence of police/suspect exchanges.

For other reasons more directly linked to the videoing process itself, the Commission expresses reservations about the widespread use of video recording of interviews (see paragraphs 70-72, page 40 of the Commission's report). These reservations are reflected in the majority Recommendation 70 that:

**Table 1.** Type of persuasive tactic used by the police in observed interrogations and number of suspects on whom tactics used. (1)

| TYPE OF TACTIC | Times Used | No. of Suspects |
|---|---|---|
| 1. Exercise of police discretion | 22 | 17 |
| 2. Provision of expert knowledge | 3 | 2 |
| 3. Influencing suspects' assessment of consequences of confessing: | | |
|   a)  Utilitarian consequences for self or others | 11 | 4 |
|   b)  Social consequences | 24 | 11 |
|   c)  Self-esteem | 45 | 27 |
| 4. Telling the suspect he has no decision to make because of: | | |
|   a)  Forensic evidence | 103 | 52 |
|   b)  Witness evidence | 172 | 64 |
|   c)  Accomplice information | 28 | 14 |
|   d)  General background information | 20 | 12 |
| 5. Use of custodial condition: | | |
|   a)  Confinement | 1 | 1 |
|   b)  Authority | 17 | 8 |
|   c)  Physical control | 0 | 0 |
| 6. Accusation or abuse | 159 | 55 |
| 7. "This is your opportunity to explain" | 38 | 25 |

**Note:** The table is based upon interrogations relating to 157 suspects. For 30 suspects (19.1 per cent) no persuasive tactics were used, in ten of these cases because the suspect, following earlier legal advice, made an immediate confession at the start of the interrogation. For 37 suspects (23.6 per cent) only one type of tactic was used, and in 21 of these cases the tactic was used on only one occasion.

(1) From Study 16, Pg 129, Table 7.1

"further research should be carried out to inform future consideration of whether video recording of interviews should be introduced on a more widespread basis".

These reports (Studies 2, 5, 8 and 16 in particular) have also criticised police interviews for the standard of the questioning and of the record produced of that interview.

## Interview Techniques

Study 16 is highly critical of police interviewing techniques. Compared with earlier quoted studies, this report finds that police officers adopt a more confrontational interviewing style with greater emphasis on securing confessions. It describes a range of manipulative and persuasive ploys that police use to effect confessions, and suggests that the form of question used could result in unreliable or wrongful confessions, and so, by implication, possible miscarriage of justice. (See tables 1 and 2).

Not surprisingly, the researcher recommends a massive and long-term police training programme for interviewing, to prevent this so-called 'unskilled' police questioning. Yet, the researchers admit that training itself will be insufficient to change police practices without an enormous turn-around in police institutional philosophy. This philosophy underpins the police acting out their role in the current adversarial criminal justice system and using investigation as a confrontational verification technique.

These observations open a plethora of resource issues, in addition to the obvious philosophical concerns about the appropriateness of present police practices and the need for fundamental structural changes in the criminal justice system, changes which may not have been within the scope of the Royal Commission to recommend.

In the face of the potentially far-reaching consequences of the research findings, two comments may be pertinent. First, the research in Study 16 is a bi-product of research on custodial legal advice; the interview sample, though large (n=157), was drawn entirely from that small sub-set of police interviews undertaken in the presence of a legal representative. The sample is not, therefore, representative of police interviews as a whole, and so, on methodological grounds alone, further investigation is warranted. Still, it is highly probable that further studies on police investigation methods will find evidence of the same 'questionable' techniques, though probably on a different scale from this study.

Secondly, criticism of police interviewing seems to be widespread. Even within this set of research reports, the views expressed in Study 16 are unique only in their

**Table 2.** Type of question form used by police, number and proportion of investigations in which used (1)

| Question Form | | Interrogations n=157 | |
|---|---|---|---|
| | | n | % |
| 1. Establishment | To establish a relationship with suspect | 31 | 19.7 |
| 2. General Information | Usually about the suspect, but not directly linked to offence | 52 | 33.1 |
| 3. Offence – Focused Information | Focused on a particular offence | 72 | 45.9 |
| 4. Leading Question | To persuade suspect to give a particular answer | 31 | 19.7 |
| 5. Statement Question | An interrogatory tagged to the end of a statement, inviting the suspect to accept the whole statement | 50 | 31.8 |
| 6. Explanation of Evidence | Confronting suspect with incriminating evidence, but without reference to a specific offence | 62 | 39.5 |
| 7. Supported Accusation | Direct accusation supported by evidence | 30 | 19.1 |
| 8. Legal Closure | Attempting to make suspect self-identify into a legally significant category, without first establishing the offence | 56 | 35.7 |
| 9. Police Opinion | Seeking to persuade suspect to adopt a police opinion or statement | 53 | 33.8 |

(1) From Study 16, p.139, Table 7.4

stridency. If completely scrapping the present adversarial basis of the criminal justice system is unacceptable, a less radical approach to changes in police interviewing techniques needs to be sought, one which can co-exist with the existing adversarial criminal justice system.

In Study 8, criticisms of aggressive police interviewing techniques also occur. Although both Studies 16 and 8 note the passivity of the 'interview witness' – the responsible adult for juveniles or the legal representative for adults-in intervening against police pressure to prevent their 'charge' from possible self-incrimination, Study 8 differs from Study 16 in acknowledging the adversarial system of criminal justice and recognising that persuasive interview techniques may well be legitimate. Yet, it contemplates a compromise change in interview practice to place clear limits on the use of persuasive and manipulative techniques at interview, while still preserving the present adversarial criminal justice system. Directing interview training towards information gathering rather than to manipulative questioning should eventually foster change in the emphasis of interviews.

Even this compromise carries with it resource-costs on police forces through significant increases in training costs; innumerable hours spent in policy development devising the new limits to apply to persuasive interviews techniques; and in explaining the new procedures to working police officers to forestall their reluctance, resistance and perception that such moves will further shift the balance of fairness in apprehending criminals towards the suspect. The Commission did not explore or recommend on these issues.

**Interview summaries**

After the interview comes the interview report (or summary) and the research studies soundly criticise these also. Study 2 found that half of the summaries, a proportion increasing with interview length, fail as a record of the interview, either because they are misleading or lack detail. Study 8, which examines juvenile cases found by listening to the interview tapes, that in 20% of the cases when the suspect was released with a caution, he had failed specifically to admit his guilt, contrary to the indication of the report.

Yet, despite their criticisms, the results are broadly supportive of the police position, and conclude that the defects in interview summaries arise from the police role in Britain's adversarial criminal justice system. The studies argue that the process of summarisation is a selection process. Notwithstanding individual variations between officers in skills at summarising, the prosecutorial role of the police in the criminal justice system will mean that they (the police) cannot be expected to take a defence or even a neutral stance in preparing summaries.

The implication of this finding is that no lawyer, defence or prosecution, should, for case preparation purposes, take the interview summary as a sufficient record of the interview and should always listen to the tapes. While this advice arises from research observations of the weaknesses in the summary reports, it is asking of both counsel no more than work that they should undertake as part of good legal practice.

Police summaries, the researcher observes, fail because police do not and cannot, because of their professional perspective, prepare a report that best meets the needs of all summary users. Yet, police responsibility for summary reports has become entrenched in the present criminal justice system. To transfer that role to the lawyers will deliver to them a resource cost which they claim they cannot sustain within present budgetary allocations (Study 2). However, in the words of the report, 'while the task remains the responsibility of the police service', it is inevitable that problems will arise.

Civilian input into preparing interview summaries may mitigate the problem, and Study 2 looked at schemes in Northamptonshire and in Hampshire where civilians were involved in preparing interview reports under police supervision. The research found that these schemes did not generate significantly better reports than were produced by forces with only police input into the summary preparations.

The main argument for increased civilian involvement has been savings in police resources. Yet, overall these may be slight. Civilian staff, chosen for their precis skills, would still require considerable police supervision and direction. Besides, resources must be expended on civilian training on the legal aspects of summary preparation. Furthermore, given the continuing police direction of the interview summary process, civilian involvement in summary preparation would seem unlikely to alter the prosecution bias inherent in the reports.

The Royal Commission recommended (see paragraph 79, page 42 of the Report) that the Home Office, in consultation with other interested parties, should explore further, by experiment where appropriate, four options for handling interview reports, viz

- dispensing with interview reports;
- maintaining the status quo;
- passing the responsibility for the preparation of interview reports to the CPS; and
- transcribing interviews in full

to establish the best practice method of producing interview reports for the future.

# 5. Right to silence

The issue of the right to silence during police interviews is canvassed in Studies 10, 16, and 19. Study 19 merely surveys the incidence of detainees invoking the right to silence, without attempting to draw conclusions from or explain causal links in the evidence.

Studies 10 and 16 attempt an analytical approach to detainees' silence during interview. Neither paper holds much joy for the working police-officer hoping for some change to this provision. And in accord with the research findings, Recommendation 82 states:

> "The majority of us believe that adverse inferences should not be drawn from silence at the police station and recommend retaining the present caution and trial direction."

Study 10 finds "… that reform of the right to silence would have a limited effect in enhancing the prospects of convicting guilty offenders in only a very small proportion of cases" while Study 16 concludes "… that the right to silence should be strengthened rather than further weakened or attenuated".

These conclusions are reached on the basis of different perspectives. Thus Study 10, from an objective examination of the evidence, concludes that there is a scant case for refining the right to silence because there is unlikely to be any great difference in outcome for convictions if the right to silence were abolished.

Study 16 takes a more philosophical approach. The criminal justice system, it notes, is adversarial. This has many implications including the nature of police investigative philosophies and the relationship that exists between the police, individuals and communities. It is the responsibility of the prosecution, not of the detainee, to make a case against an accused. The right to silence is embedded in the structure of this system, and, the paper argues, not an add-on extra. Accordingly it cannot be removed without a philosophical rethink of the whole criminal justice structure, or, at least it cannot be removed from the suspect unless it is also denied to the prosecution. (The researchers of Study 16 observed that police officers selectively use silence when interviewing detainees.) The effect of this argument complies with the majority view of the Royal Commission which was stated in Recommendation 83 as:

> "… it is when but only when the prosecution case has been fully disclosed that defendants should be required to offer an answer to the charges made against them at the risk of adverse comment at trial on any new defence they then disclose or any departure from the defence which they previously disclosed."

The Royal Commission's arguments to reach their conclusions are set out in paragraphs 20-25, on pages 54-55 of the Report.

In the process of arriving at their conclusions, the research studies dismiss and confirm other commonly-held assumptions on the impediments for working police officers posed by suspects exercising their right to silence.

First, the incidence of the exercise of the right to silence was observed to be low in these studies. Study 10 was based on a sample of 848 police interviews 'collected' from 1986 to 1988. Only 4.5% of the total invoked their right to silence, defined to mean a refusal by the detainee to answer questions relating to his own involvement.

However, in accord with the widely-held belief of police officers, the right to silence was more frequently invoked when the detainee had legal representation. Thus it was that 11% of the interviewees who had legal representation were silent during questioning. This group comprised only 10% of those interviewed, but 24% of those who remained silent.

Yet in 78% of the cases in Study 16 legal representatives did not advise their clients to silence. This concurs with the survey findings in Study 19 which found that in 80% of cases legal advice did not lead to detainee silence. Further, the research suggested that while the police tended to assume that silence equated to guilt, there was more than one reason that a legally-represented detainee may choose to be silent.

- In some cases cause and effect were reversed from that generally supposed, and the suspect requested legal advice as a protection against foul play because he had already decided to be silent;

- alternatively he may have remained silent as self protection because he was concerned about the competence of his legal advice;

- the research found that in more than 60% of 'silence' cases, the silence was precautionary in the face of an information deficit by the detainee about the police case, and was a decision bound up with his historic perceptions of the police.

Although the incidence amongst "professional criminals" of invoking the right to silence was not studied, the research found that many detainees do not withstand police questioning. A statement was eventually produced from 25% of those interviews where the right to silence was at some time invoked. This outcome should be compared with the 36% incidence of statements prepared from detainees who were prepared to answer all questions put to them. It is noteworthy, however, that it was in the context of this questioning that Study 16 was critical of what it characterised as 'persuasive and manipulative police interviewing tactics' and 'inappropriate' interrogation strategies.

By contrast, Study 10 found that a detainee's denial is more effective than his silence in impeding police in following a case. In only 5% of the cases where the police tried to break down a negative response did they succeed.

Study 19 also found, in contradiction to widespread police concern, that in about 80% of cases the jury had learned of the defendant's silent response to police questioning. In addition, for the sample of cases under consideration, defendants were less likely to be acquitted if they had remained silent during interrogation than if they had answered questions.

Further, contrary to police concern, Study 10 found few cases are lost on ambush defences raised after a suspect has asserted his right to silence.

- Almost 50% of the cases set for contested trial were abandoned, some perhaps because CPS had insufficient evidence to refute defences they had been given notice would be raised in court (though this possibility is raised, not investigated).

- However for those 50% of cases that did get to court to be contested, ambush defences were raised in only 5%, and only half of these were successful.

- It is worth noting that unanticipated defences that were not defined as ambush defences were used in 8.5% of the sample of contested cases. These defences had been revealed in earlier police interviewing, and were only unexpected because police had failed to follow them up.

The wastage rate of cases prepared by the police could warrant further research. Neither it, nor its effect on police morale, has been investigated in these published study reports. The fundamental differences in outlook by police and prosecutors, and problems of their working interaction is however touched on in several of the papers. In particular, police productivity is judged on "clear-up" rate and that of the CPS on "conviction rate" of cases sent to court. Accordingly, in simple terms, the police seek enough evidence to charge, the CPS to convict. The dichotomy of institutional aims causes inter-agency tensions, and a demarcation of responsibilities between the two that owes more to historical resource distribution than logical work allocation (eg. see earlier discussions on interview statements) and offers a field-day for further researchers.

Study 16 emphasises that the right to silence is an integral component of the adversarial criminal justice system. Within that system inquisitorial information gathering sits uneasily. However, three special cases are noted in the research papers, Fraud, (see Study 14), HOLMES (see Study 5) and pro-active, rather than re-active intelligence gathering (also Study 5).

Special provisions apply to information gathering in serious fraud cases, under Section 2 of the Criminal Justice Act 1987. This provision requires witnesses, however unwilling, and despite the possibility of implicating themselves, to answer the questions of Serious Fraud Office (SFO) investigators. That clause, or the threat of it, is liberally used by the SFO to prepare cases. But still, this information is given only to SFO investigators (accountants and/or lawyers); police officers seconded to the SFO are deliberately excluded from this process because their involvement may be construed as compromising the witnesses' right to silence. Consequently, any statements made to investigators by witnesses must also be re-made to police officers to produce court evidence. However, if the witnesses' new statement is inconsistent with his earlier one, this can be brought to the attention of a court, (in contrast to police detainees silence during interview under PACE conditions). This provision is discussed in the Commission's Report (see paragraphs 28-30, page 56) and Recommendation 84 supports its continuation.

Study 5 observed that much of the effort in a HOLMES investigation is on collecting, cross-checking and corroborating information. But, by contrast to the fraud cases, the right to silence and the protections for detainees of the PACE Act are followed, while the lattice-work of information is collected. These may hinder the 'search for truth' and failure to disclose information may rebound on the individual concerned or may misdirect an investigation. There is no suggestion that police bend the rules to compensate for these and other problems in using HOLMES. There may be a case for further research to determine the extent to which the right to silence hinders such major investigations, especially during their information-gathering phase, since no evidence on this was provided in Study 5.

Study 5 does, however, comment favourably on criminal intelligence, and surveillance-based investigation as one way of overcoming some of the problems of hasty re-active policing. While 'the wrong person' is rarely charged using these methods, pro-active investigation is very resource intensive and thus, expensive. Furthermore, these techniques are not immune from claims of manipulation and malpractice, for example in keeping log books, in the evidence of police eye-witnesses, and in handling informants. But, perhaps the biggest threat to a larger-scale adoption of these methods lies with the civil rights issues. The present scale and nature of surveillance-based investigations has generated no organised civil-libertarian criticism. But a less selective use of the techniques may become the focus of more public interest and, as in some other western democracies eg Australia, ultimately may constrain police in their future use of pro-active policing techniques.

# 6. Confession evidence alone

Miscarriages of justice arising from 'false' confession evidence have led to suggestions that a police confession should not be admitted as evidence in court unless it is corroborated. [The Royal Commission did not support this view. See paragraphs 65-75, pages 64-66 of the Commission's report for their discussion of this issue.] However, Study 13 had focused on the implications of this proposal; its conclusions had favoured such a change in prosecution requirements. It urged that

> "consideration be given to the introduction of a rule to prevent the conviction of a person on the basis of confession evidence unless corroborated by independent evidence which itself points unambiguously to the guilt of the defendant or (less preferably) which connects or tends to connect the accused with the crime."

Using a 1989 sample of 524 prosecuted cases drawn from 3 different police areas, the research shows that only a slightly lower rate of prosecutions and convictions would be expected from such a policy change. Furthermore, it argues, the research results could well be an overestimate of the present effect of the change since anecdotal evidence indicates that present police practices rely less on confession evidence alone than in the survey year. It was found that with no changes in police practices, 7.8% of the sample prosecutions would fail a corroborative evidence test, or 6.7% when those cases that would fail in any event are excluded from the sample. So, from the original 524 prosecutions, 35 cases were identified that may in their present form succeed but which would fail a corroborative test. However, for 25 of these cases, further evidence either was available but not pursued, or could have been collected. This leaves only 10 cases (or 1.9% of the original set of 524) that would fail to be prosecuted because of reliance on confession evidence that *could not be* as distinct from *was not* corroborated.

To gain those 25 prosecutions (almost 1 in 20 of the sample) for which further evidence must be collected under a corroboration requirement entails a resource cost to the police. Most of the evidence 'available' yet 'uncollected' was forensic and probably therefore not pursued because of its cost. Case selection and the amount of work devoted to a particular case entails a loose resource cost benefit decision. Fifty percent of all potential cases are already wasted, ie not brought to court for whatever reason. That additional resources were not expended on these cases suggests that the police consider them, perhaps subconsciously, to be close to the margin of their resource cost/benefit balance. To impose a higher resource cost on them may well mean that they will not be pursued. This raises the question of whether a new corroboration requirement for confession evidence will lead to a higher wastage rate of cases before prosecution, rather than to failures of prosecution. That wastage rate may approach the 6.7% of cases implicated by the research as not viable under a corroboration requirement, rather than effect merely 1.9% of cases as the researcher suggests. The research identified 3 reasons for which the police curtail investigations so resulting in weaknesses in evidence

- a confession is obtained, so police perceive no need for further investigation;

- for resource reasons, viz the investigation is becoming too costly;

- poor work practice, viz failure, for no apparent reason, to check all available sources.

To overcome weaknesses in evidence gathering developed from police procedures, the research recommends the following changes in investigative practice.

- Police evidence-gathering techniques and any related training or supervisory requirements within the police should be revised to ensure that advantage is routinely taken of investigative opportunities and that relevant and admissible evidence is collected and preserved;

- standard systems of documentation should be developed to assist the police in providing a comprehensive account of cases which track in chronological order the investigative strategies pursued;

- police reports to prosecutors should in all cases include specific reference to the steps taken to obtain evidence, the evidential product of each of those steps, the additional investigative steps which are available, and the reasons why those additional steps have not been pursued; and

- police reports to prosecutors should include specific reference to problems which are anticipated if witnesses are required to provide direct oral testimony at court.

While such changes would provide the prosecution with a more complete understanding of police strategies and of all possible available evidence, again, as with so many of the recommendations in these papers, they involve resource costs to the police. In this example, the costs will accrue from more investigation and more paperwork. These recommendations point once more to the question of how much preparatory work the police should do for CPS, and where the balance of responsibility and resource commitment between CPS and the police lies. When a deficiency in preparation of cases exists, it is often easier to recommend that police practices are changed to cover the deficiency, than it is to focus on which player in the criminal justice system will improve its service by the mooted changes. Most of these suggested changes in practice fall into the category of improving the efficiency of the CPS, rather than the Police in fulfilling their statutory obligations, and police forces may not enthusiastically embrace the prospect of an increased work load without appropriate resource compensation for the benefit of another agency.

# 7. Conclusion

There are well over a thousand pages in the research reports commissioned by the Royal Commission, and this paper has touched on only some of the issues that they canvas. For example, it has not reported on the studies as diverse as the "Role of Police Surgeons", or "Directed Acquittals in Crown Court".

Three general issues recur, however, throughout the reports:

- specialist vs generalist policing;
- the latent resource cost of most proposals/recommendations; and
- the differences in practice between forces, resulting in some recommendations having a far greater potential relevance for selected forces.

Throughout the research papers, the theme of specialisation recurs in recommendations for specialist investigators, specialist prosecutors etc. Needless to say, these pressures and the tradeoffs they entail are familiar to modern police management. Specialisation should yield benefits from enhanced officer-effectiveness in the specialist role, but these gains must be balanced against the disadvantages of 'down-time' lost to general policing, and the lesser possible flexibility in manpower management both in the shorter and longer term.

At the same time, most suggested changes in police practices will have resource implications. For example, training costs money. A recommendation for specialist training (as in the case of the 'mental health' fitness for interview of a suspect) will have a different budgetary impact, depending on whether the recommendation applies to all officers or to a specialist group.

The resource cost outcome for the various proposals will differ between forces depending on present manpower-management and operational practices. If, for example, the notion of specialist custody officers referred to in Section 2 was universally adopted, as a policy change it will affect different forces differently. Forces that already employ specialist custody officers will need to make no change in their procedures, whereas there may well be changes to, for example, shifts and training with subsequent resource cost implications, for those forces without specialist custody officers. Research studies generally fail to predict the aggregate effect (including all costings) of a proposal, if force differences exist, so warranting further investigations before a policy decision, mindful of all the implications, can be made.

Police practices are criticised in the research papers, but so too are those of other groups. For example, defence lawyers are shown to be motivated, in the main, by financial rather than service considerations, and the competence with which they handle their pre-trial work is brought into question.

The reports have, *inter alia,*

- supported some opinions widely held by the police eg. that detainees with legal representation are more likely to invoke the right to silence; but also

- refuted other commonly held views eg that lawyers invariably advise their clients to remain silent;

- identified a range of police organisational practices needing reform, for example, in
  – identifying vulnerable detainees
  – supervision of investigations and
  – interview report writing;

- recommended new practices to compensate for the perceived present weaknesses. Most of these recommendations would entail resource costs if implemented, but consideration of costings was outside the researchers' brief.

Nonetheless, not all the reports chose to offer solutions to problems identified. For example, the research into police interview report writing identified weaknesses in present practices but did not set out to canvas satisfactory alternatives.

And finally, it must be emphasised that these papers, although commissioned by the Royal Commission are the work of independent researchers. The recommendations, arising from the research findings have no policy standing. They are recommendations of the researchers, and distinct from those of the Commission. In the case of the issue of confession evidence alone, for example, the Commission's recommendations contradict those favoured by the researcher of Study 13.

# Appendix A

## ROYAL COMMISSION ON CRIMINAL JUSTICE
### Terms of Reference

**From the Royal Warrant, the terms of reference of the Commission are:**

To examine the effectiveness of the criminal justice system in England and Wales, in securing the conviction of those guilty of criminal offences and the acquittal of those who are innocent, having regard to the efficient use of resources and in particular, to consider whether changes are needed in:

i.     the conduct of police investigations and their supervision by senior police officers and in particular, the degree of control that is exercised by those officers over the conduct of the investigation and the gathering and preparation of evidence;

ii.    the role of the prosecutor in supervising the gathering of evidence and deciding whether to proceed with a case and the arrangements for the disclosure of material, including unused material, to the defence;

iii.   the role of experts in criminal proceedings, their responsibilities to the court, prosecution and defence and the relationship between the forensic science service and the police;

iv.    the arrangements for the defence of accused persons, access to legal advice and access to expert evidence;

v.     the opportunities available for an accused person to state his position on the matters charged and the extent to which the courts might draw proper inferences from primary facts, the conduct of the accused and any failure on his part to take advantage of an opportunity to state his position;

vi.    the powers of the courts in directing proceedings, the possibility of their having an investigative role before and during the trial, and the role of pre-trial reviews; the courts' duty in considering evidence, including uncorroborated confession evidence;

vii.   the role of the Court of Appeal in considering new evidence on appeal, including directing the investigation of allegations;

viii.  the arrangements for considering and investigating the allegations of miscarriages of justice when appeal rights have been exhausted.

and make recommendations.

# Appendix B

## LIST OF ROYAL COMMISSION RESEARCH PAPERS

### No 1:   A report on the administration of criminal justice in the pre-trial phase in France and Germany by Leonard Leigh and Lucia Zender

This report deals with law and practice in France and Germany. It provides sufficient detail on the two systems to serve as a context for discussion of the operational practices in the two jurisdictions, with particular stress on supervised investigation.

### No 2:   Preparing records of taped interview

This study, critical of the quality of police records of interview, indicates that about fifty per cent of a sample of 200 records fail either because they are faulty or lack detail. The proportion of unsatisfactory records of interview increases with interview length.

The paper concludes that lawyers, both defence and prosecution, should listen to the taped record rather than rely on summary as a record of the police interview.

### No 3:   Role of legal representatives at police stations by John Baldwin

This study focuses on the role of legal representatives involved in 182 of the sample of 600 interviews. Results showed these representatives to be passive and compliant during interviews, and as perceiving their role to be conciliatory and acquiescent.

### No 4:   Supervision of police investigations in serious criminal cases by John Baldwin and Timothy Maloney

This CID based study identifies two distinct models of supervision:(1) major enquiries supervised by senior officers who managed the operation, and (2) smaller enquiries involving small numbers of officers working as a team, where the supervisor's main input is his name on a final report.

The researchers criticise the latter model because small group performance depends on the competence and integrity of the individuals concerned and incorporates too few checks. The main recommendation from the report is to strengthen supervision by enhancing the role of sergeants.

## No 5:   The conduct and supervision of criminal investigations by Mike Maguire and Clive Norris

Another CID based study, this one examines the conduct and supervision of criminal investigation in divisional CID offices, major incident rooms and regional crime squads. In every case the study outlines the organisational and supervisory structures, the dominant and investigative style and the kinds of evidence typically sought. The study seeks out the areas most vulnerable to error or malpractice and assesses the existing supervisory and regulatory mechanisms for preventing deliberate or mistaken miscarriages of justice. The report is highly critical of 'CID' culture.

The report recommended, inter alia, that forces establish a quality control unit which may randomly check any detective activity, including procedural and legal compliance of the investigation, as well as officer-effectiveness.

## No 6:   The role of police surgeons by Graham Robertson

This study describes and assesses the work of police surgeons and how it impinges on the operation of the criminal justice system.

It found that between one thousand five hundred and two thousand doctors are employed as police surgeons. The largest share of their work relates to intoxification. The study examined the role of police surgeons in assessing whether prisoners are fit to be detained and/or to be interviewed. The criteria to assess fitness for interview varies between doctors.

The researcher recommends that where no forensic purpose is met by medical examination in custody, that the prisoner be treated as a temporary NHS patient with all the implied doctor-patient confidentiality. Also, it was recommended, that the costs of specialist training for police surgeons should be met by the employing Force.

## No 7:   Devising and piloting an experimental version of the notice to detained persons by Isabel Clare and Gisli Gudjonsson

This study, by using an experimental group of 100 adult subjects, tested detainees' understanding of their rights while in police detention as 'explained' in the notice to detained persons. It was found that only 40% fully understood the present notice.

An experimental notice was trialled and a much higher level of understanding observed.

The researchers concluded that the experimental Notice is a considerable improvement on presently used versions. They recommend that the direct questions on a detainee's need for an appropriate adult be adopted in police stations as soon as possible, and that, after amendments, the experimental Notice be piloted in police stations to ascertain its value in practice.

### No 8:   The conduct of police interviews with juveniles by Roger Evans

This research analyzed factors associated with confessions and denials during police interviews with juveniles.

It was critical of police interviewing techniques including oppressive questioning; it further observed that the adult present with the juvenile in the interview room rarely intervened, leaving the juveniles unprotected and exposed to the police interview tactics.

The study found that twenty per cent of suspects cautioned or informally warned, made no clear admission of the offence concerned, contrary to Home Office guidelines.

Like Report 2, this paper suggested that taped interviews should be checked against the summary record.

### No 9:   The ability to challenge DNA evidence by Beverley Steventon

This study aimed to evaluate the problems a defence lawyer may face both pre-trial and at trial, when dealing with a case involving DNA profiling evidence.

The research confirms that, despite the wide acceptance of the technique, and its value when identification is an issue, there is scope for dispute over interpreting DNA profiling results. It is therefore crucial, the researchers conclude, for the defence to obtain an independent evaluation of the prosecution's evidence.

The researcher recommends that the courts must ensure the defence are notified of the existence of DNA evidence in sufficient time pre-trial for a suitable expert to be hired and to carry out all the necessary testing for the defence. Legal aid should be granted automatically for one expert assessment of the prosecution work and DNA evidence should only be admissible when an appropriate expert is available to the defence.

Without these conditions, the researcher suggests, the prosecution evidence will be unduly prejudicial and should be excluded.

APPENDIX B

## No 10:  The right to silence in police interrogation: a study of some of the issues underlying the debate by Roger Leng

The researcher attempts to test some of the assumptions underlying arguments for reform and to quantify the arguments that, by involving the right to silence,

(1)  a significant number of criminals avoid being charged

(2)  a significant number of criminals ambush the court trial by producing a new defence.

The study found that the true right to silence (ie a detainee remaining silent on all issues pertaining to himself) is rarely exercised and about half of those who exercise it are convicted. Further, true ambush defences are very rare and only about 50% are successful when raised.

The study concludes that proposed modifications to the right to silence would enhance the prospects of convicting guilty offenders in only a very small proportion of cases.

## No 11:  The role of forensic science evidence in criminal proceedings by Paul Roberts and Chris Willmore

This paper provides an in-depth account of the collection and presentation of forensic evidence in criminal proceedings. The research examined twenty four cases where post-committal forensic evidence had been obtained by the Bristol and Avon CPS. The method of case selection must, therefore, raise doubts over whether this sample of forensic science cases is representative.

The study concluded that the true strengths and limitations of forensic science are not adequately stressed and that there is scope for errors to pass undetected and potential challenges to be missed by the defence. The potential for error resides in all cases in which forensic science evidence is utilised. The authors advised defence solicitors, in particular, to be aware of this fact.

## No 12:  Persons at risk during interviews in police custody: the identification of vulnerabilities by Gisli Gudjonsson, Isabel Clare, Susan Rutter and John Pearse

The research attempts to assess suspects psychologically to establish characteristics and vulnerabilities prior to interview by the police.

About fifteen per cent of the sample fulfilled the PACE criteria for the presence of an appropriate adult during interview, significantly in excess of the four per cent identified by the police. While police were very good at identifying most disabled vulnerable suspects, they were less adept at identifying mental handicap and depressive mental illness.

The recommendations include those for more police training to identify more readily vulnerable individuals, self-identification of vulnerable individuals under questioning, and specialist custody officers.

### No 13: Corroboration and Confessions. The impact of a rule that no conviction can be sustained on the basis of confession evidence alone by Mike McConville.

Based on a sample study, this research examines the issues raised in the debates on confession and corroboration evidence focusing on:

(1)　the extent to which existing prosecutions depend on the suspect's confession

(2)　the extent to which confession based cases could be buttressed by further evidence

(3)　the ease with which further evidence can be obtained

(4)　the trials and number of cases for which corroborative evidence is unavailable.

The study concludes that a corroboration rule would impose higher evidential requirements on police, and some but not a major decline in cases brought to conviction.

The researcher found strongly in favour of a decisive move away from reliance on extra judicial confession evidence alone.

### No 14: The investigation, prosecution and trial of serious fraud by Mike Levi.

This discursive examination of fraud centres on the key issues involved in the investigation, prosecution and trial of serious fraud cases.

The report distinguished the modus operandi and powers of the various key agencies that investigate fraud and questions the values of the criminal justice system in relation to fraud.

It finds that the police/lawyer team-work principle in the Serious Fraud Office could be useful in other major crime investigations.

## No 15: Ordered and directed acquittals in the Crown Court by Brian P Block, Claire Corbett and Jill Peay

A qualitative, in-depth study of a sample of 100 non-jury acquittals to see what proportion could have been avoided, either by obtaining further evidence or by discontinuing prosecution. Of the sample, the researcher found that 43% could or might have been avoided.

A raft of recommendations, mainly applying to CPS procedures, were made, but including the observation that it would be of great benefit if police Crime Support Groups (Administrative Support Units) were made more accountable to the CPS. The research does not specify whether financial responsibility should accompany a shift in administrative responsibility.

## No 16: Custodial legal advice and the right to silence by Mike McConville and J Hodgson with M Jackson and E MacCrae

This research study set out to examine the circumstances in which solicitors and their staff advise police detainees to remain silent or to co-operate with police during interrogation.

The researchers conclude that the right to silence has meaning in terms of structural features of the criminal justice process rather than in matters personal to the suspect.

## No 17: Review of the appeal process by Kate Malleson

This review examines the practices of the Court of Appeal to determine how it interprets and applies its powers. The study is based on a review of the first 300 appeals against conviction considered by the Court in 1990, and the first 102 successful appeals in 1992.

It was found that the Court of Appeal rarely hears fresh evidence, considers the existence of a "lingering doubt" or orders a retrial. The incidence of retrials in the study rose between 1990 and 1992 and applications for leave to appeal by counsel were significantly more successful (about a 50% success rate) than non-counsel led applications (less than a 20% success rate).

It recommended that the Court should be enabled to carry out independent investigations on the conduct of the trial, the pre-trial investigation, forensic evidence and fresh evidence raised on appeal. Further, the report recommended that defence counsel error should be a valid grounds for appeal.

APPENDIX B

**No 18:   Information and advice for prisoners about the grounds for appeal and the appeals process by Joyce Plotnikoff and Richard Woolfson**

Based on a survey of 2242 prisoners who had recently completed 28 days since conviction or sentence, this study set out to determine how well newly convicted prisoners were advised of their right to appeal.

The provision of advice was found to be variable with more than half of solicitors found incorrectly to advise their clients that the Court of Appeal could impose a more severe sentence on appeal.

Recommendations were made to change procedures in the Courts and in the prisons to ensure an improvement in the quality of advice that prisoners receive.

**No 19:   Crown Court Study by M Zander and P Henderson**

All participants (except witnesses and victims) in all cases in all but three Crown Courts in the country during a fortnight early in 1992 were sampled for this detailed appraisal of views and opinions on the working of the Crown Court. (There were 3191 cases).

The study draws no conclusions but lists findings covering a diversity of issues from arrest to conviction. Thus the study records, for example, whether the defendant invoked his right to silence, and whether the jury knew of this, as well as whether there was a statistical association between the thrust of the judge's summing up and the outcome of the case.

**No 20:   Ethnic Minorities and the Criminal Justice System by Marian Fitzgerald**

A careful literature-based study, assembling and analysing the key findings from existing research on ethnic minorities at each stage in the British criminal justice system.

**No 21:   Human Factors in the Quality Control of CID Investigations**

This study is based on a sample supplied by investigating officers of 60 CID case studies involving some type of quality control failure. The researcher aims to describe and categorise types of system errors.

The most common causes of error were found to be

- failure to foresee and to take account of circumstances which should have been foreseen

- errors in processing information

- errors in communication.

Besides recommending that further information be gathered on causes of error, the research recommended that police acknowledge in training, supervision and inter-agency dealings that human error exists in policing.

## No 22:   The questioning and interviewing of suspects outside the police station by Stephen Moston and Geoffrey Stephenson

The PACE Act placed a series of controls on interviews with suspects within police stations. But even after the 1990 revision, the Codes of Practice applicable to non-station interviews remain confused and ambiguous, and their application depends crucially on a distinction between questioning and interviewing.

This study considers a sample of 641 detainees who were interviewed in a police station. It found that 31.5% had been questioned before being brought to the police station, and that 8.1% had been interviewed before arriving at the police station.

The researcher found that interrogation was a process, and not a single incident occurring in a police station. To acknowledge this, allow inclusion of the complete interaction between detainee and police officer, and to diminish the importance of the formal station interview, the researcher recommended that all officers carry portable tape recorders and record the entire interaction with both suspects and witnesses. The researcher also cast doubt on the benefit of video recording of station interviews.

## Unnumbered:   Criminal justice systems in other jurisdictions edited by N Osner, A Quinn, G Crown

This volume is a compendium of summaries describing the criminal justice systems in 14 other jurisdictions. Those covered are Australia (by state), NZ, US, Canada, Israel, the Republic of Ireland and eight European countries.

# Police Research Series Papers

1.  **Video Taping Police Interviews with Suspects – An Evaluation.** John Baldwin. 1992. vi +31pp. (0-86252-885-2)

2.  **Effective Shift Systems for the Police Service.** Richard Stone, Tim Kemp, Bernard Rix and George Weldon. 1993. vii+40pp. (0-8652-746-5)

3.  **Opportunities for Reducing the Administrative Burdens on the Police.** Paul Cresswell, Graham Howarth, Mike Dolan, John Hedges.1993. xiii+55pp. (1-85893-097-9)

4.  **Investigative Interviewing Courses for Police Officers: an Evaluation.** Barry McGurk, Michael Carr and Debra McGurk 1993 vii+36 pp (1-85893-0847)

Printed in the UK for HMSO. Dd8382585   11/93.